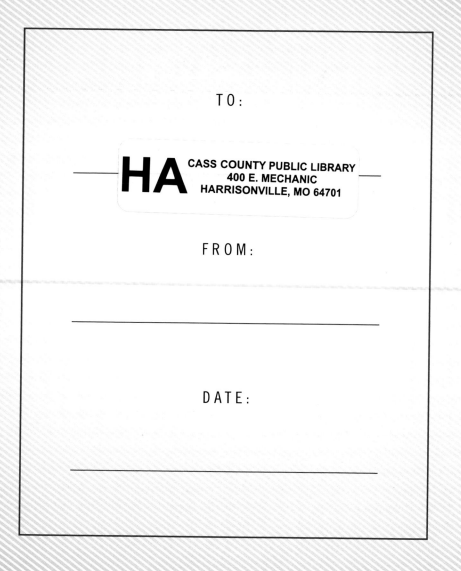

TO:

FROM:

DATE:

Copyright © 2014 Meadow's Edge Group LLC
ISBN: 978-1-4336-8361-9
Published by B&H Publishing Group, Nashville, Tennessee

Dewey Decimal Classification: B
ZIGLAR, ZIG \ QUOTATIONS \ ATTITUDE (PSYCHOLOGY)--QUOTATIONS
Publishing Category: Christian Living/Spiritual Growth/Inspiration

CONTENT FOR THIS BOOK WAS GLEANED FROM THE FOLLOWING SOURCES:

Inspiration 365 Days a Year by Zig Ziglar. Copyright 2008 by Simple Truths,
LLC. All rights reserved. www.simpletruths.com. Used by permission.

Confessions of a Happy Christian by Zig Ziglar. Copyright
1978. Used by permission of the licensor, Pelican
Publishing Company, Inc. www.pelicanpub.com.

The Universal Library (www.ul.cs.cmu.edu)

Additionally, *Zig: The Autobiography of Zig Ziglar* was vital to verifying
biographical details of Mr. Ziglar's life. This book was co-published in 2002
by WaterBrook Press and Doubleday, both divisions of Random House, Inc.

Other quotes were gleaned from Zig Ziglar speeches delivered
at two Future of the Industry Conferences, presented by
the Christian Booksellers Association (CBA).

Unless otherwise noted, Scripture quotations are taken from the Holman Christian
Standard Bible® (HCSB®), Copyright © 1999, 2000, 2002, 2003 by Holman Bible
Publishers. Used by permission. Holman Christian Standard Bible®, Holman CSB®,
and HCSB® are federally registered trademarks of Holman Bible Publishers. Other
translation: New International Version (NIV), copyright © 1973, 1978, 1984
by International Bible Society. Used by permission. All rights reserved.

Packager Development: Meadow's Edge Group LLC
Editorial Development: Todd Hafer
Designed by ThinkpenDesign.com

1 2 3 4 5 6 7 8 9 · 19 18 17 16 15 14

LIFE WISDOM

QUOTES FROM

ZIG ZIGLAR

INSPIRE TO BE GREAT!

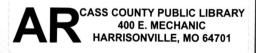

TABLE OF CONTENTS

INTRODUCTION

*Good news from a distant land is
like cold water to a parched throat.*

Perhaps TV's *60 Minutes* said it best. When it comes to motivating people, "Zig Ziglar is a legend in the industry—the Bill Gates, Henry Ford, and Thomas Edison of enthusiasm."

Many people talk up the power of positive thinking. Zig lived it. Born Hilary Hinton Ziglar in rural Coffee County, Alabama, he was the 10th of twelve children. His father died when he was only five, and he was raised by his widowed mother in Yazoo City, Mississippi.

Zig, who described himself as "an unusually small child," grew up during the heart of Depression, and he battled serious illness as a youngster, passing the first grade only through the selfless intervention of a loving teacher, Mrs. Dement Warren.

Despite his bleak upbringing, Zig thrived on the encouragement of people like Mrs. Warren and his mother, Lila Ziglar. The latter loved to serve him wisdom in tasty bites of prose or poetry. "The person who won't stand for something," she told him, "will fall for anything."

Such memorable homespun wisdom would become a hallmark of Zig's motivational speeches and best-selling books later in his life.

Zig served in the U.S. Navy at the end of World War II, and then attended college for a while. He was not a great student, and he eventually dropped out to sell cookware door-to-door for the WearEver Aluminum Company. His career started slowly, but through determination and discipline, he became a top salesman.

During his career, he sold everything from cookware to life insurance, from timber to fine china, and from nutritional supplements to cleaning products.

Fueling his rise as a successful salesman was the wisdom and motivational fire of self-help speakers and writers.

Inspired to share what he was learning, Zig began to give talks at local churches and Rotary Club meetings. As his skill and reputation grew, he became a Dale Carnegie instructor and, later, a featured speaker at sales conferences and motivational seminars for Mary Kay Cosmetics.

Before long, he launched out on his own and became a go-to speaker for large corporate retreats and conferences. His clients included a "Who's Who" of Fortune 500 companies.

His "Success Rallies" and "Born to Win" seminars attracted thousands. During his peak years, his speaking fee topped $50,000. He shared the stage with United States Presidents Ford, Reagan, and Bush, as well as

General Norman Schwarzkopf, Secretary of State Colin Powell, and radio icon Paul Harvey. The National Speakers Association presented him with its highest honor, The Cavett Award.

Zig wrote twenty-seven books, including the best-selling classics *See You at the Top* and *Secrets of Closing the Sale*.

The star of many of his books and speeches was Jean "The Redhead" Abernathy, his wife of more than sixty-six years. He said, "If it had not been for the fact that by the day she encouraged me, and at night she prayed for me, there's no question in my mind that I would not have enjoyed even a small fraction of the success that God has privileged me to attain."

Zig Ziglar died on November 28, 2012, at age eighty-six. His legacy of motivation and encouragement lives on.

*"Go into all the world
and preach the gospel to
the whole creation."*

MARK 16:15

*People often tell me
that motivation doesn't last,
and I tell them that bathing
doesn't either. That's why
I recommend it daily.*

ZIG ZIGLAR: UP CLOSE AND PERSONAL

Who is like the wise person, and who knows the interpretation of a matter? A man's wisdom brightens his face.

ECCLESIASTES 8:1

I don't have an **ALARM** clock; I have an **OPPORTUNITY** clock.

My mother was my greatest TEACHER. *She taught us with "sentence sermonettes." One was:*

"Your children pay more ATTENTION *to what you* DO *than what you* SAY."

When I talk about my wife, I always call her the REDHEAD. She's a decided redhead— meaning that one day she just DECIDED to be a redhead.

Had you asked me if I really **LOVED** my wife **PRIOR** to knowing Jesus Christ, I emphatically would have assured you I did, because, to the best of my ability, I did love my wife. But once **CHRIST** entered the picture . . . I entered into a new and far **GREATER DIMENSION** of love. I loved her before in my own way; I love her today in the way that our Lord would have me love her. The relationship is so much more **BEAUTIFUL**.

The Redhead and I are more **IN LOVE** than ever. We **TALK** more than ever. We **DO** more things together. It's fairly typical for us to spend an **HOUR** together over breakfast.

The first twenty-seven years of our marriage were financially very difficult. But the Redhead never wavered. She always gave me complete SUPPORT. *If it had not been for the fact that by the day she* ENCOURAGED *me, and at night she* PRAYED *for me, there's no question in my mind that I would not have enjoyed even a small fraction of the* SUCCESS *that God has privileged me to attain.*

To avoid PROCRASTINATION, *write your schedule out the night before, including precisely when you are going to start. My first year in sales, I struggled desperately. I knew I had to do something. So I made an appointment with myself. Every morning at 9, regardless of the weather or anything else, I was knocking on the doors. That year, I finished number two out of 7,000 salespeople. But here's something that's fascinating about that: Not one week did I finish in the top 20, but I had* STEADY BUSINESS. *To this day, I have my daily priorities all lined out. Without a* PLAN, *nothing is going to work out.*

I hate to be **NEGATIVE**. As a matter of fact, I **WON'T** be negative.

My huge obstacles in life became **BUILDING BLOCKS**. I am the 10th of twelve children. I grew up in the heart of the Depression. My mom had a 5th grade education, but incredible wisdom. My dad died when I was five. But God put, always, a **CERTAIN PERSON** in my path to fill the void.

My first-grade teacher, back in the 1930s, is a classic example. I had every childhood disease, and I missed four months of school. Now, when you miss four months of school, chances of you passing are pretty slim. But Mrs. Dement Warren, twice a week, drove out to our house. I'd go out to her car, and she spent an hour teaching me and bringing me up to speed. Had she not done that, I would have failed the first grade. And had I failed the first grade, I would have been drafted out of high school in World War II. As it was, I was able to finish high school on schedule and qualify for the Naval Air Corps' V5 program—and they always started you in college. I never would have seen the inside of a college door . . . had it not been for Mrs. Warren.

Here is one thing I learned later in life: At forty-five, I had a serious ego problem. I thought I had all the answers. I had a FALSE PRIDE. And the bottom line is: That was a serious HANDICAP. When I finally realized that, I started listening to the WISDOM of people who had balance in life. And that's when I started my Wall of Gratitude.

I have in my office what I call my **WALL OF GRATITUDE**. There are twenty-six men and women who God placed in my path, from childhood, at specific times. And each one has played a huge role in my life. Because I've had so much help and because I really do believe you can have everything you want in life, if you will help enough other people get what they want—that's why I do what I do. A **HELPING HAND** can change a life.

For twenty-four years of my adult life, I had a **WEIGHT PROBLEM**. I was on a roller coaster—up and down, up and down, and up and down. Finally I figured it out: I needed to lose just **ONE AND 9/10THS OUNCES A DAY**, on average, every day for **TEN MONTHS**. Then, at the end of the ten months,

I would have lost the thirty-seven pounds I needed to lose. In order to accomplish that, I started **EATING SENSIBLY** and **EXERCISING REGULARLY**. Not trying to run marathons, but just making a **REGULAR HABIT**. Decades later, I weigh exactly today what I weighed when I lost those thirty-seven pounds back in 1972.

If the AH-HA *I get when I'm reading is not already reduced into one or two sentences, I'll take the essence of what I've read and chunk it into easily remembered* BITES *of information. That information is what becomes* "QUOTABLE." *You would not sit still for me to read every book I've ever read to you. But if you're the least bit like me, you'll jump at the chance to bypass all the churning and scoop the cream right off the top. That is what quotes are . . . the* CREAM *of our learning.*

My advice to
public speakers:
PREPARE extensively
every time . . .
and be **FUNNY**.

The Redhead and I,
we celebrate
HONEYMOONS,
not anniversaries.
ANNIVERSARIES
can be boring, but
not honeymoons.

Before the day is over, the redhead and I will HUG *twenty times. We just* ENJOY *each other, and all that affection and intimacy—and every day the repetition of "I sure do love you. You're very special to me." I'm so lucky. Some men wait till age forty or fifty to get a* TROPHY WIFE. *I got mine when I was just twenty. I'm always still astonished how* BEAUTIFUL *she is after living with me for more than fifty-some years.*

*I never judge
a day by the*
WEATHER.

You can ask my wife:
On my **WORST** days, I'm
still **HIGHER** than a kite.

The right quote can INSPIRE *people to* CHANGE *their ways*

FINDING TRUE SUCCESS

*The one who understands a matter
finds success, and the one who
trusts in the Lord will be happy.*

PROVERBS 16:20

I define **SUCCESS** as having acquired **SOME** of the things that money will buy and **ALL** of the things that money won't buy—while maintaining **BALANCE** in your life.

I LIKE *what money buys. I like to wear nice clothes, live in a nice house, drive a nice car. Play golf at the country club. Love to take that beautiful redheaded wife of mine out to nice restaurants. All of those things cost money. But I* LOVE *the things money* WON'T *buy.*

Money bought me the house, but it won't buy me a HOME. *It'll buy me a companion, but it won't buy me a* FRIEND. *It'll buy me a good time, but it won't buy me* PEACE OF MIND. *It'll buy me a bed, but it won't buy me a good night's* SLEEP.

What you GET by achieving your goals is not as important as what you BECOME by achieving your goals.

Don't count the things you **DO**. Do the things which **COUNT**.

You can have **TOTAL SUCCESS**
when you balance your physical,
mental, and spiritual life—
as well as your personal,
family, and business life.

Success is the
MAXIMUM
UTILIZATION
of the ability
that you have.

It's not where you START—*it's where you* FINISH *that counts.*

If I made **MILLIONS** and that pretty redhead of mine left me, what a **MISERABLE** human being I'd be.

Or, if I was **SUCCESSFUL** in what I did in the business world but my kids ended up on drugs, or rebellious and in prison, I certainly would not have considered myself to be a **SUCCESS**.

In America, we have become **GREEDY**. We are bombarded with so many ads that say, "You gotta have this car! You gotta wear these clothes! You gotta take this vacation trip! You gotta have that second home at the beach," and all of these absurd things. Over the years, I have noticed this—that if **STANDARD OF LIVING** is your number-one objective, your quality of life almost never improves. But if **QUALITY OF LIFE** is your number-one objective, standard of living invariably goes up. That kinda contradicts what a lot of people believe.

HAPPINESS *is not a when or a where; it can be a* HERE *and a* NOW. *But until you are happy with* WHO YOU ARE, *you will never be happy because of* WHAT YOU HAVE.

When you clearly understand that success is a PROCESS, not an event, you are encouraged to follow the right process to create the SUCCESS you are capable of having.

Success Procedure:
Run your day by the
CLOCK and your life
with a **VISION**.

You can have **EVERYTHING** in life you want if you will just help enough other people get what **THEY** want.

Help OTHER PEOPLE *be successful. That's what it's all about. It's not about* YOU.

Be **GRATEFUL**.
Believe.
Try.

INTEGRITY MATTERS

I will pay attention to the way
of integrity . . . I will live with a
heart of integrity in my house.
PSALM 101:2

The most important **PERSUASION** tool you have in your arsenal is **INTEGRITY**.

As a Christian, I always ask myself the question, "What would JESUS do?" If you're not a Christian, you can ask, "What is the right thing to do?"

Make sure, as you make decisions, that it's the RIGHT THING to do for everyone concerned.

I love to quote my mother:

"Tell the TRUTH *and tell it ever, costeth what it* WILL;

for he who HIDES *the wrong he did, does the* WRONG *thing still."*

We hear people say, "Well, you know, everything is relative. There's nothing that's black and white." Which is **ABSURD**. I've never yet talked to a business man or woman who has said they would hire an **ACCOUNTANT** or a **TREASURER** who said he or she was just relatively honest. I've never come home from an out-of-town trip and had that pretty redhead of mine ask me if I had been "relatively faithful." There are some things that are **RIGHT**, and some things are **WRONG**. So you build relationships on **TRUST**.

You might not be what you **SAY** you are, but what you say, you **ARE**.

Every CHOICE
you make has an
END RESULT.

You can actually measure the PROGRESS *of a nation based on the level of* TRUST *within that nation. The loss to the typical American family during all of these corporate scandals [of the early 2000s] was $60,000 per family. And the stock market lost over 3 trillion dollars in value. All of that can be laid at the feet of* GREED *and lack of* CHARACTER.

The **FOUNDATION STONES** for a **BALANCED SUCCESS** are honesty, character, integrity, faith, love, and loyalty.

Integrity is simply doing the **RIGHT THING**. A lot of times, people look at what is the profitable thing. People with integrity are more **SUCCESSFUL**, because with integrity you do the right thing, and there is no guilt attached to you. With integrity, you have **NOTHING TO FEAR** because you have nothing to hide. Think about that. If a person has fear and guilt removed from his shoulders, he is **FREE** to be his very best. She's free to be her very best. That gives them a leg up. They don't have to look over their shoulder. They can continue to **FOCUS** on the moment, in **PREPARATION** for the future.

In our country, you are free to **CHOOSE**, but the choices you make **TODAY** will determine what you will be, do, and have in the **TOMORROWS** of your life.

A pleasing PERSONALITY
*helps you win friends and
influence people. Add*
CHARACTER *to that formula
and you keep those friends
and maintain the influence.*

If you tell someone you're going to be there at 9:00, don't you **DARE** show up at 9:01. Do the things you tell people you are going to do.

Honesty and integrity are absolutely **ESSENTIAL** for success in life—all areas of life. The really **GOOD** news is that anyone can develop **BOTH** honesty and integrity.

FAMILY MATTERS

"As for me and my family,
we will worship Yahweh."

JOSHUA 24:15

Fellas, let me tell you something about your WIVES: They resent it when you ignore them all day, then give them your undivided attention when the lights go out at night. They want that HUG when all you've got on your mind is a hug. They want AFFECTION. They want you to put your arm around them, hold their hand. Tell them how BEAUTIFUL they are. Tell them how much you LOVE them. And they want it MORE than once a day.

Many **MARRIAGES** would be better if the husband and the wife clearly understood that they are on the **SAME SIDE**.

We need to **PREPARE** all of our children to work and prosper in the world we live in today. When you awaken your children in the morning, do it **GENTLY**, kindly. End each day **PRAYERFULLY** and lovingly, and **ENCOURAGE** them. When you make a mistake, **APOLOGIZE** for it. Remember, the **EXAMPLE** you set is so important.

As a Christian, I am totally committed to the belief that when a child sees a parent bow in OBEDIENCE *to a Higher Authority, the child is taught, by example, how to* RESPECT *authority. So they will listen respectfully and follow through on what the parent says, the teacher says, the police person says, and right on down the line. That gives them a* HUGE *leg up on life.*

Be the RIGHT KIND *of person. You've got to have that character base. Be* STRAIGHTFORWARD *and disciplined. You've got to do the right thing. That includes doing the right thing for your* FAMILY.

People who have good relationships at **HOME** are more effective in the **MARKETPLACE**.

With the family, we start by understanding that men and women are dramatically **DIFFERENT**. Despite the fact that we say that, we often treat each other as if men and women are **ALIKE**. I often laughingly tell audiences, "Ladies, your husband—he doesn't give a hoot about what's on television. All he wants to know is what **ELSE** is on television."

I say to the ladies, "When your husband has been knocked flat on his back, when he's lower than a snake's belly, when his self-image is down to zero, if at that specific time, you will become the AGGRESSOR, *make it crystal clear that despite the fact that he's suffered a setback—maybe he's lost his job that he's had for twenty years—you find him irresistibly* ATTRACTIVE, *there is nothing that will build a man's* EGO *and* CONFIDENCE *like that will."*

Husbands, if you treat your wife like a THOROUGHBRED, *chances are good you won't end up with a nag. Wives, if you treat your husband like a* CHAMP, *chances are even better that you won't end up with a chump.*

Here's another thing that I emphasize: Women have a different **INTELLIGENCE** than men do. They instinctively and intuitively know things that us men don't have a clue to. Women have **INSIGHTS** that men don't have. Husband and wife, put them together and you've got an **INCREDIBLE** team. Husband and wife are **SMARTER** than either one of them alone.

Kids don't make up 100 percent of our **POPULATION**, but they do make up 100 percent of our **FUTURE**.

Parents, spend that TIME *with your children early on, certainly by the time they are three-years-old.* TALK *with them,* LOVE *them unconditionally, and* READ *to them.* MODEL *for them what is right and what is wrong.* TEACH *them the importance of* OBEDIENCE.

I believe that being successful means having a BALANCE *of success stories across the* MANY AREAS *of your life. You can't be truly successful in your* BUSINESS *life if your* HOME *life is a shambles.*

LEADERSHIP FROM THE INSIDE OUT

*You should be an example to the
believers in speech, in conduct,
in love, in faith, in purity.*
1 Timothy 4:12

The best CEOs, the ones that build their companies successfully, are very HUMBLE. *The humble person has open* EARS *and an open* MIND *and will take legitimate feedback, and* SEEK *it, for counsel and direction and advice.*

In leadership, there are some leaders who develop **FOLLOWERS**. But there are some leaders who develop other **LEADERS**. The greatest **JOY** that comes to any human being is to watch someone else's **SUCCESS**. That's where real joy comes from.

MOTIVATION is the spark that lights the fire of **KNOWLEDGE** and fuels the engine of **ACCOMPLISHMENT**. It maximizes and maintains **MOMENTUM**.

ENCOURAGEMENT
is the fuel on which
HOPE *runs.*

The greatest GOOD we can do for anyone is not to share our wealth with them, but rather to REVEAL their own wealth to them. It's astonishing how much TALENT and ABILITY rest inside a human being.

With leadership, everything starts with **INTEGRITY**. And **COMMUNICATION SKILLS** are absolutely critical.President Eisenhower observed that leadership is getting other people to do what you want them to do, because they **WANT** to do it.

If you can't be generous when it's **HARD**, you won't be generous when it's **EASY**.

Every obnoxious
ACT *is a* CRY
for help.

People were designed for
ACCOMPLISHMENT,
engineered for SUCCESS,
and endowed with the
seeds of GREATNESS.

HARD WORK
IS WORTH IT!

*There is profit in all hard work, but
endless talk leads only to poverty.*

Proverbs 14:23

Success is
DEPENDENT
on the glands—
SWEAT *glands.*

You don't **PAY** the price for success; you **ENJOY** the price for success.

It was **CHARACTER**
that got us out of bed,
COMMITMENT that moved
us into action, and
DISCIPLINE that enabled
us to follow through.

There are no
TRAFFIC JAMS
on the extra mile.

When you are TOUGH *on yourself, life is going to be infinitely* EASIER *for you.*

In your hands you hold the seeds of **FAILURE** or the potential for **GREATNESS**. Your hands are **CAPABLE**, but they must be used— and for the **RIGHT THINGS**—to reap the **REWARDS** you are capable of attaining. The choice is **YOURS**.

It's better to flip hamburgers than sell drugs. For many kids—who have not been taught **DISCIPLINE** but who have been raised on television—that kind of job is the first time they have been learning **RESPONSIBILITY**, how to deal with people effectively, the importance of money and why it is different when you've earned it versus Mom and Dad giving it to you. How you develop that **PERSONALITY**, how you gain work habits. How you become **SELF-SUPPORTIVE**.

You want to talk about flipping HAMBURGERS? We've done an awful lot of training in the fast-food industry, and I know a number of young men and women, less than twenty-five years old, who are earning more than $50,000 dollars a year and are driving company cars. Now that ain't all bad! One of the fast-food companies I do a lot of work with—they have people who are actually earning one, two, three, four, and even five MILLION dollars a year. At this particular time, flipping hamburgers is the only kind of job a lot of people can get. But if they do that, there are the chances of being DISCOVERED. CEOs are always looking for highly motivated, enthusiastic, committed, and responsible people. You never know WHO you might be serving.

REPETITION *is the mother of learning, the father of action, which makes it the architect of* ACCOMPLISHMENT.

Give it your **BEST SHOT**.
Don't go through the motions
and get fired from a job
you are over-qualified for.
Every job, every day—
FULL SPEED ahead.

We deny our **TALENTS** and **ABILITIES** because to acknowledge or to confess them would commit us to **USE** them.

A lot of people
QUIT LOOKING
for work as soon as
they find a JOB.

This I know beyond any reasonable doubt: REGARDLESS of what you are doing, if you pump long enough, hard enough, and enthusiastically enough, sooner or later the EFFORT will bring forth the REWARD.

Where you **START** is not as important as where you **FINISH**.

When you do the things you **NEED** to do when you need to do them, the day will come when you can do the things you **WANT** to do, and when you want to do them.

When you DO more than you are paid to do, the day will come when you will be PAID more for what you do.

EXPECT *the best.*
PREPARE *for the worst.*
CAPITALIZE *on*
what comes.

It's not what you've **GOT**; it's what you **USE** that makes a difference.

YESTERDAY *ended last night.* TODAY *is a brand-new day and it's* YOURS.

THE QUEST FOR KNOWLEDGE

*Instruct a wise man, and he will
be wiser still; teach a righteous
man, and he will learn more.*

PROVERBS 9:9

I encourage everyone to **RE-READ** books several times so that they can glean every bit of **APPLICABLE INFORMATION**. Re-reading fixes ideas in your mind that might otherwise slip away. I also suggest that readers **HIGHLIGHT** the words that inspire, motivate, encourage, and move them to new **ACTION** and **THOUGHT**.

When you add NEW INFORMATION *to what you already know, your creative* IMAGINATION *can mingle the information and present you with an entirely new* PERSPECTIVE *on the subject at hand.*

When your
VOCABULARY
goes up, your IQ
goes up. So become
a WORD *student.*

I read for the **AH-HAS**, the information that makes a light bulb go off in my mind. I want to put information in my mind that is going to be the most **BENEFICIAL** to me, my family, and my fellow man: financially, morally, spiritually, and emotionally.

There are quotes that **LIFT YOU UP** and quotes to bring you **BACK TO EARTH**.

With good quotes, you remember WHO *said it,* WHAT *the circumstances were, and that it had an* IMMEDIATE IMPACT *on your thinking.*

I seldom read anything that is not of a FACTUAL nature, because I want to invest my time wisely in the things that will IMPROVE my life. Don't misunderstand; there is nothing wrong with reading purely for the joy of it. Novels have their place, but biographies of famous men and women contain information that can CHANGE LIVES. Dr. Norman Vincent Peale's The Power of Positive Thinking *changed my THINKING. The Bible changed my BELIEVING. Ultimately, what I have read has changed my BEING.*

When I can hook up
old information with
new information, the
COMBINATION of the two
creates **PERSPECTIVES**
that could never have been
achieved otherwise. New
information makes new and
fresh ideas **POSSIBLE**.

When I **LEARN** something, I always ask the question: "How can I **APPLY** this?"

Reading has been the FUEL *of my motivation. It has changed the* DIRECTION *in which I have traveled, and it has enhanced my* CREATIVE IMAGINATION *more than any other activity I have ever pursued.*

Read your BIBLE. *It's easy to understand if you'll ask the Author to* GUIDE *you in it. He is always* AVAILABLE.

I'm in my **EIGHTH DECADE** of living, and I still read **SEVERAL HOURS** a day.

A **NARROW MIND** and a **FAT HEAD** invariably come on the **SAME PERSON**.

Some quotes make you SMILE, *and some will create more* QUESTIONS *than you might care to think about. But good quotes make you* THINK, *and thinking is an exercise that will enhance and improve your* FUTURE *immensely.*

If you **APPLY** what you learn to your life, I can honestly say I'll see you at the **TOP**.

ATTITUDE FUELS ACTION!

Bright eyes cheer the heart; good news strengthens the bones.

PROVERBS 15:30

You were BORN *to win,*
but to be a winner,
you must PLAN *to win,*
PREPARE *to win,*
and EXPECT *to win.*

If you want to reach a **GOAL**, you must **SEE** the reaching in your own mind before you actually **ARRIVE** at your goal.

Never say anything
NEGATIVE about yourself.
If **WE** don't see ourselves as
"fearfully and wonderfully
made," **WHO** will?

The most important OPINION *is the one* YOU *have of yourself, and the most* SIGNIFICANT *things you say all day are those things* YOU *say to yourself.*

When your GOALS are clearly defined and intelligently set, you have, in essence, taken a MAJOR STEP toward programming your left brain. That frees your right brain to be its CREATIVE best.

Most people who **FAIL** in their dreams fail not from lack of ability but from lack of **COMMITMENT**.

You can make **POSITIVE DEPOSITS** in your own economy every day by **READING** and **LISTENING** to powerful, positive, life-changing content and by **ASSOCIATING** with encouraging and hope-building people.

Life is TOO SHORT *to spend your precious time trying to convince a person who wants to live in doom and gloom to do otherwise. Give lifting that person your best shot, but don't hang around long enough for his or her bad attitude to pull you down. Instead, surround yourself with* OPTIMISTIC *people.*

The way you see your
FUTURE *determines*
your thinking today.
Your THINKING
today determines your
performance today. Your
PERFORMANCE *in*
the todays of your life
determines your FUTURE.

Avoid **STINKIN'** thinkin'!

Evidence is conclusive that your **SELF-TALK** has a direct bearing on your **PERFORMANCE**.

Most Americans honestly believe AMERICA *is the most powerful nation on earth, but actually the most powerful nation is* IMAGI-NATION.

You cannot climb the LADDER OF SUCCESS *dressed in the* COSTUME OF FAILURE.

If you don't **SEE YOURSELF** as a winner, then you cannot **PERFORM** as a winner.

Among the things you can **GIVE** and still **KEEP** are: your **WORD**, a **SMILE**, and a **GRATEFUL HEART**.

CONFIDENCE *is going after Moby Dick in a* ROWBOAT, *and taking the tartar sauce with you.*

Everyone has **SOMETHING** to **SMILE** about!

FACE ADVERSITY WITH COURAGE AND WISDOM!

Pay close attention to your life and your teaching; persevere in these things, for by doing this you will save both yourself and your hearers.

1 Timothy 4:16

Failure is an EVENT, *not a person. So* REGARDLESS *of what happens to you along the way, you must keep on going and doing the* RIGHT THING *in the right way. Then the event becomes a reality of a* CHANGED LIFE.

Failure is a
DETOUR, not a
DEAD-END STREET.

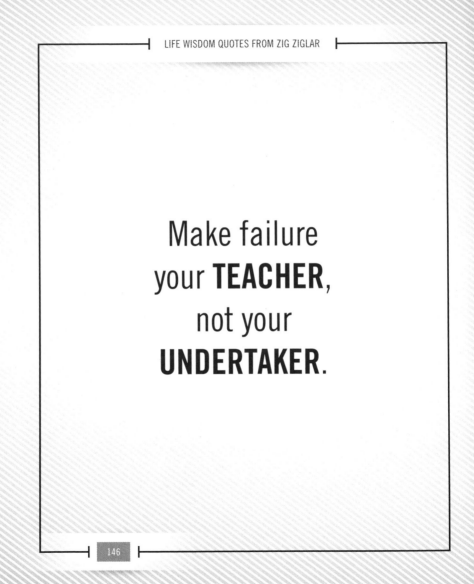

Make failure
your **TEACHER**,
not your
UNDERTAKER.

If you LEARN *from defeat, you haven't really* LOST.

Sometimes
ADVERSITY *is*
what you need to face
in order to become
SUCCESSFUL.

There is **NOTHING** you will ever face that you and God can't handle. The Lord promises us He will give us the **GRACE** to bear **WHATEVER** burden comes our way.

The **PROBLEM** might not be your fault, but it is your **RESPONSIBILITY** to do something about it. Don't blame somebody else. **ACCEPT** your responsibility and do the **BEST** you can.

There is no way we can know
WHAT *tomorrow holds,*
but we do know
WHO *holds tomorrow.*
You don't have to sit up
at night and WORRY,
because God is going to be
up ALL NIGHT *anyhow.*

If you wait until all the lights are GREEN *before you leave for town, you will stay at* HOME *for the rest of your life.*

The truth is that **FEAR** is one of the greatest inhibitors of **PERFORMANCE**.

A **GOAL** casually set and lightly taken is freely **ABANDONED** at the first obstacle.

Regardless of your LOT *in life, you can build something* BEAUTIFUL *on it.*

The God who **MADE** you can **MAKE** you over.

FAITH MATTERS

*How happy is the man who
has put his trust in the Lord.*

Psalm 40:4

Tragically, there are literally millions of people who know the **NAME** of Jesus Christ, but who know nothing of the **LOVE** and **SAVING GRACE** of Christ as Lord and Savior. Many people think of Christ as the Savior who takes instead of the Savior who **GAVE** His life to give us our lives.

Jesus came to earth prepared to FORGIVE us for our mistakes, asking only that we TRUST Him, BELIEVE in Him, and ASK for that forgiveness. Then He not only forgives, He FORGETS. That's the Jesus I love.

I shed far more TEARS *nowadays than I did before I turned my life over to Jesus Christ, but they are usually tears of* JOY *and* VICTORY *and not of bitterness or defeat.*

If you haven't met Satan face to face, it's because you are running in the **SAME DIRECTION**.

My favorite definition of a **CHRISTIAN**: a person who leads someone to **JESUS CHRIST**.

I'm confident that for every [speaking] engagement I lose by WITNESSING, the Lord gives me two to take its place. I'd be less than honest if I didn't admit I like the Lord's ARITHMETIC.

*If God would have
wanted us to live in
a* PERMISSIVE *society,
He would have given us the
Ten* SUGGESTIONS, *not the
Ten* COMMANDMENTS.

Christ doesn't **RESTRICT** our freedom. He **EXTENDS** it. A guardrail on a ship gives you **FREEDOM** to walk the edge of the deck and look more closely at the water. The guardrail on a beautiful mountain overlook gives you the **FREEDOM** to go to the very edge and view God's scenic wonders with the confident assurance that you won't slip and fall.

Mankind is all too often inclined to **TAKE CREDIT** for his accomplishments, but when things go wrong, he **BLAMES** God.

When anyone buys my services as a speaker, they buy me at my very best for that occasion. My BEST EFFORT *comes when I turn the talk over to the* LORD. *It would be* UNTHINKABLE *for me not to make reference in some way to Jesus Christ, because I would not be at my* BEST.

It is my PRIVILEGE *to share the love of our Lord with a lot of people and have others share their love of the Lord* WITH ME.

Suppose a person who did not know Jesus were to follow you for a week, and then follow one of Satan's disciples for a week. Based on what he **SAW IN YOU** as far as love, joy, happiness, and peace of mind, would that person follow Satan, or would he follow our **LORD**?

Your Christian attitude is **CONTAGIOUS**. Is yours worth **CATCHING**?

I found that virtually all the extremely SUCCESSFUL *people, if they're not with Jesus Christ, at least [they] are following biblical principles. When you do that, you can grow* TREMENDOUSLY.

I think HUMOR *is one of the great* GIFTS *of life, and I believe our Lord is happy with any humor that* GLORIFIES *both God and man.*

Serving Jesus Christ is the most **EXCITING** experience any human could **EVER** have.

*Now may the God who gives
endurance and encouragement
allow you to live in harmony
with one another.*

Romans 15:5

ACKNOWLEDGMENTS

Thank you, to the team at Simple Truths, LLC, and to Sally Boitnott, from Pelican Publishing's Rights and Permissions department, for helping to make this book possible. Your kindness and graciousness are exemplary.

Grateful acknowledgment is also due to *The Quote Verifier: Who Said What, Where, and When* by Ralph Keyes (2006, St. Martin's Press), and to *The Public Domain: How to Find & Use Copyright-Free Writings, Music, Art & More* (copyright 2008 by Stephen Fishman, published by Nolo). These references have proved to be vital sources for quote attribution and accuracy, on this and many other books.

If you enjoyed reading this book and would like to share its impact on your life, we would like to hear from you. Please send your comments via email to: meadowsedgegroup@gmail.com or write us at:

Meadow's Edge Group
P.O. Box 6947
Siloam Springs, AR 72761

Additional Life Wisdom books:

Available at bookstores everywhere or go to www.BHPublishingGroup.com for further information.